Napkin Tricks
by Susan Bonser

ISBN-13: 978-1505211382

ISBN-10: 1505211387

All rights reserved. No portion of this book may be reproduced without express written permission of the author.

All photographs and text in this book were produced by Susan and David Bonser. All rights reserved ©2014. Write to us at
P.O. Box 204, Aspers, PA 17304 or email susan.bonser@gmail.com

Other books by this author:
Create Your Digital Portfolio, The fast track to career success
Heartnuts
Heartnuts How To
Life With Cushman, A Cushman Colonial Creations Memoir
Standing in the Footsteps, Images of Gettysburg Then and Now

Our websites: adamscountyjournal.com and acreativelifebook.com
Instagram: adamscountyjournal
Facebook: adamscountyjournal

Contents

5 The Fortune Teller
9 The Sleeping Bunny
12 The Squirrel
15 The Snail
18 The Rose
22 The Dog*
24 Birdie in a Nest
28 The Fish
31 The Dancing Girl
34 Dollie
37 Twins in a Hammock*
39 Butterfly
42 Long Haired Girl
45 Bunny Puppet*

My mother performed the first napkin trick I recall. She had a knack for entertaining children—even restless children around a dinner table. The next napkin trick I remember wa at a fancy restaurant. The waiter made me a Fortune Teller out of my dinner napkin.

Quick and Easy!

Napkin Tricks

If you ever sat through a restaurant meal, wedding, anniversary or any occasion where a special meal is served, you have had waiting time—a time that can seem unendurably long to a child. If your kids are bored by crayons and puzzle books, there are slim pickings for amusement on a restaurant table—until you discover what can be done with a cloth table napkin.

Children of all ages will get a kick out of the figures you make, and want to learn to make them themselves! An indispensible skill for moms, dads, grandparents—anyone who has kids around with time on their hands.

Instead of encouraging your kids to tune out of the social potential around a restaurant table by playing with electronic devices, engage them in fun, play and conversation by making things with the napkins.

Tip: Practice these tricks ahead of time to perfect your technique. Bring your Napkin Tricks book with you to try new ones and share the fun!

Susan Bonser

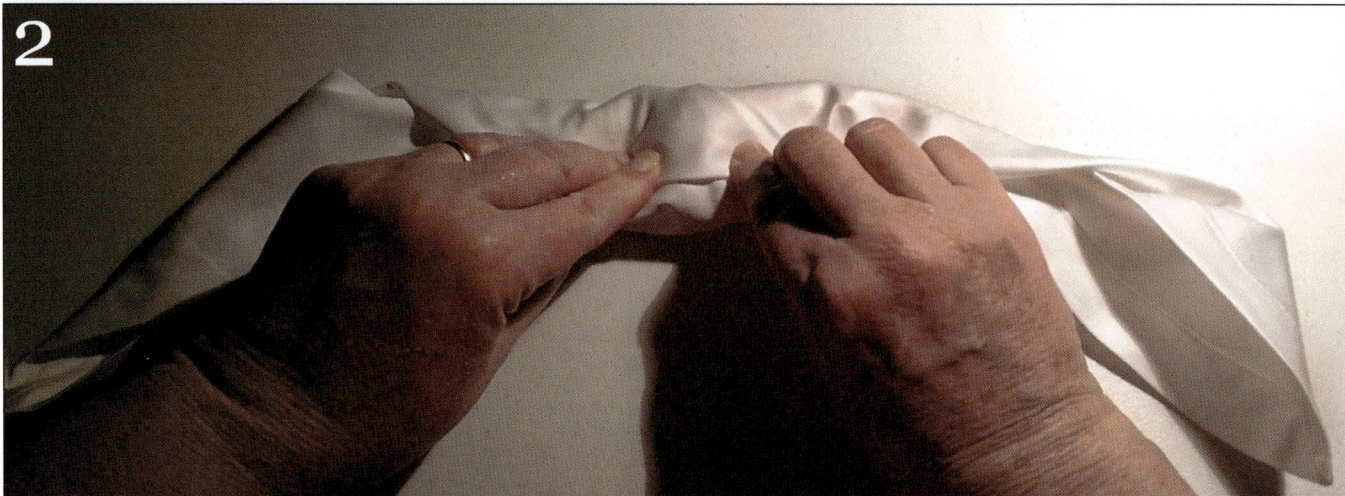

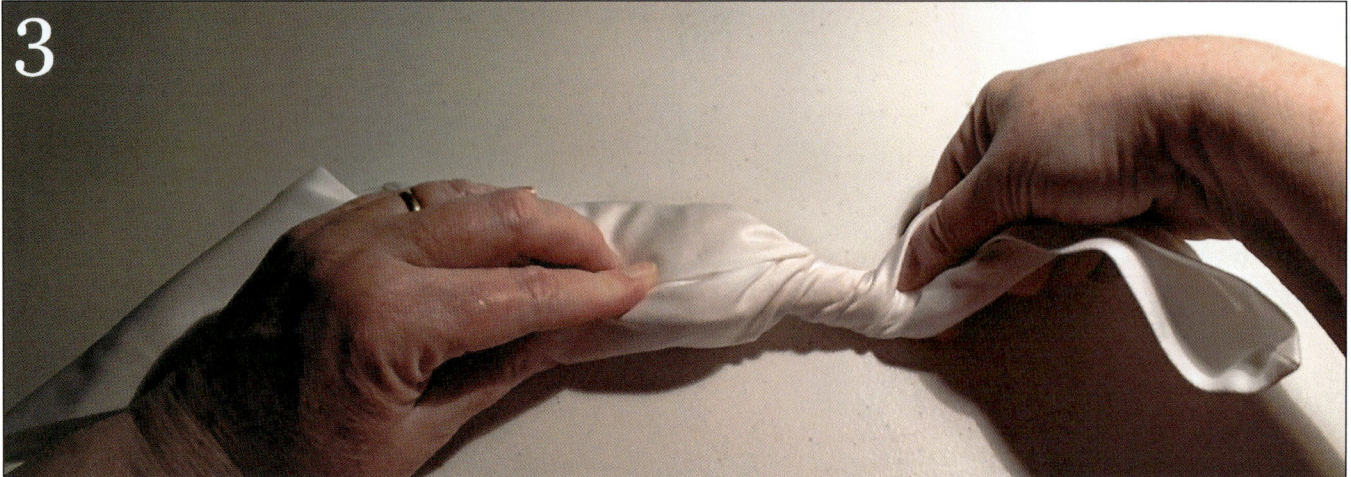

1. Tie opposite corners into a square knot. The knot gives dimension to the head.

2. Roll the sides over the knot smoothly. This will become the back of the head.

3. Twist the fabric on the right below the knot to define the chin of the head

6 Napkin Tircks

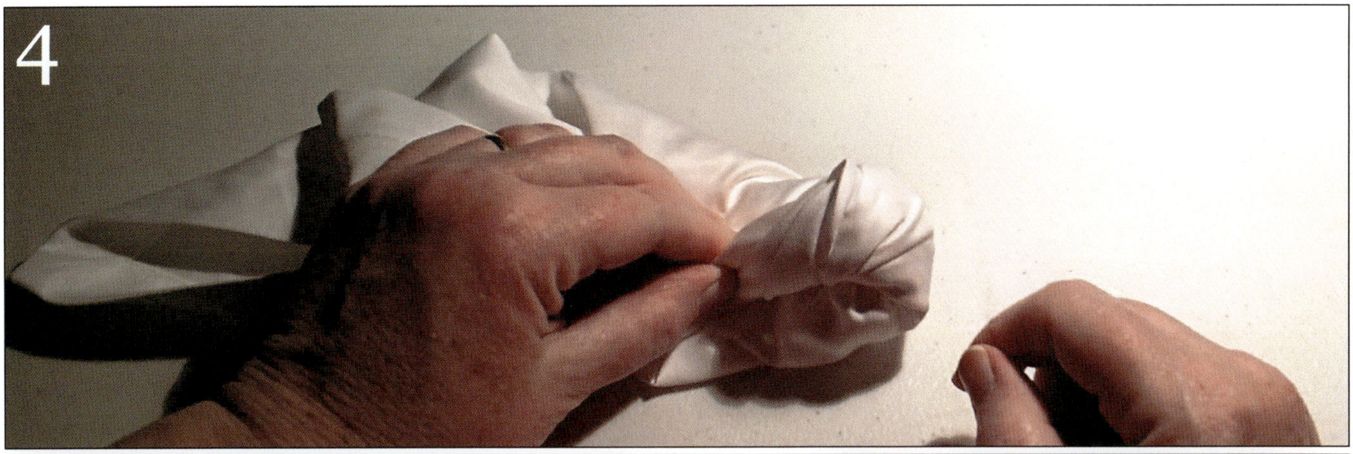

4. Bring the twisted fabric up behind the head.

5. Flip the napkin over, now it is face up. Start to twist the top of the head to create the first part of the turban.

6. Tuck the end of the turban at the back of the head under the twist securely.

Napkin Tricks 7

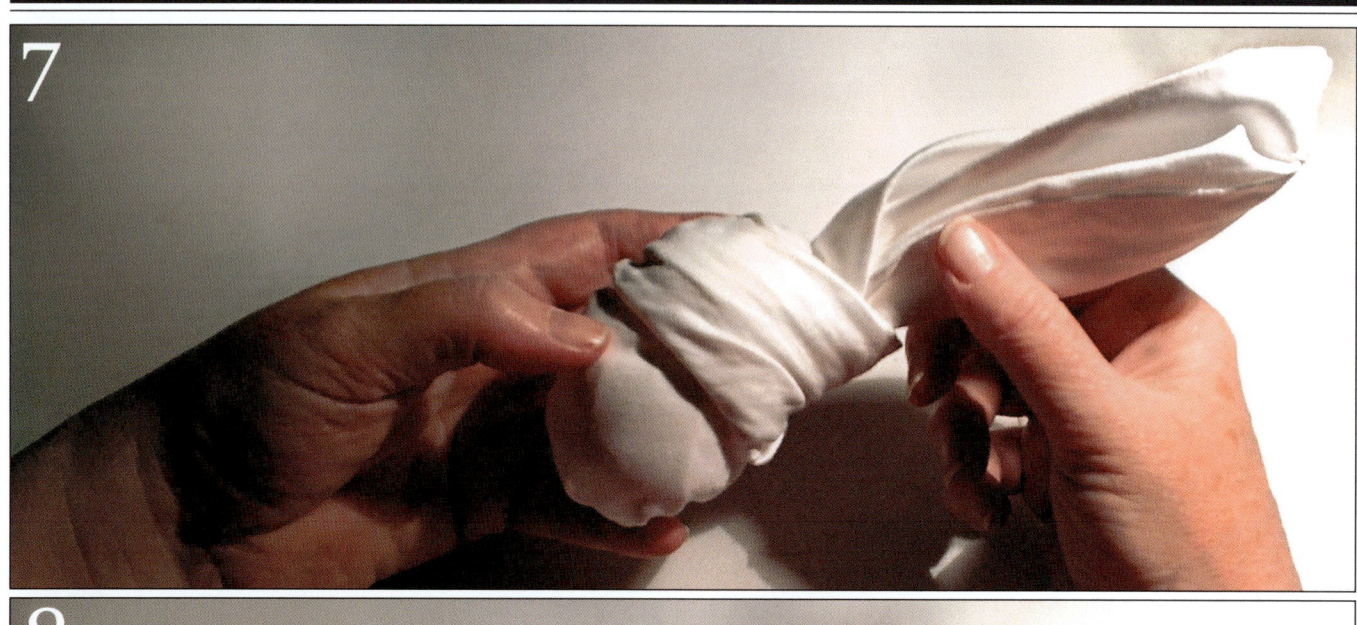
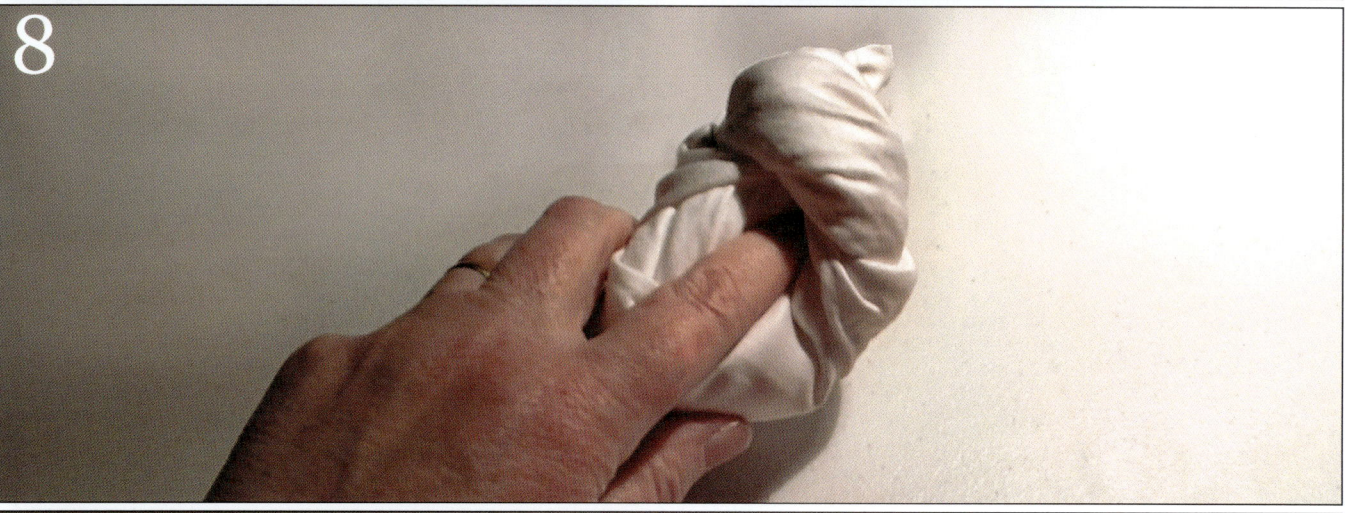

7. Twist the remaining piece of napkin the complete the turban. Secure the end.

8. Place your finger in the back of the head under the turban.

9. Ask the Fortune teller questions that can be answered with a nod "Yes" or a shake of the head "No".

8 Napkin Tircks

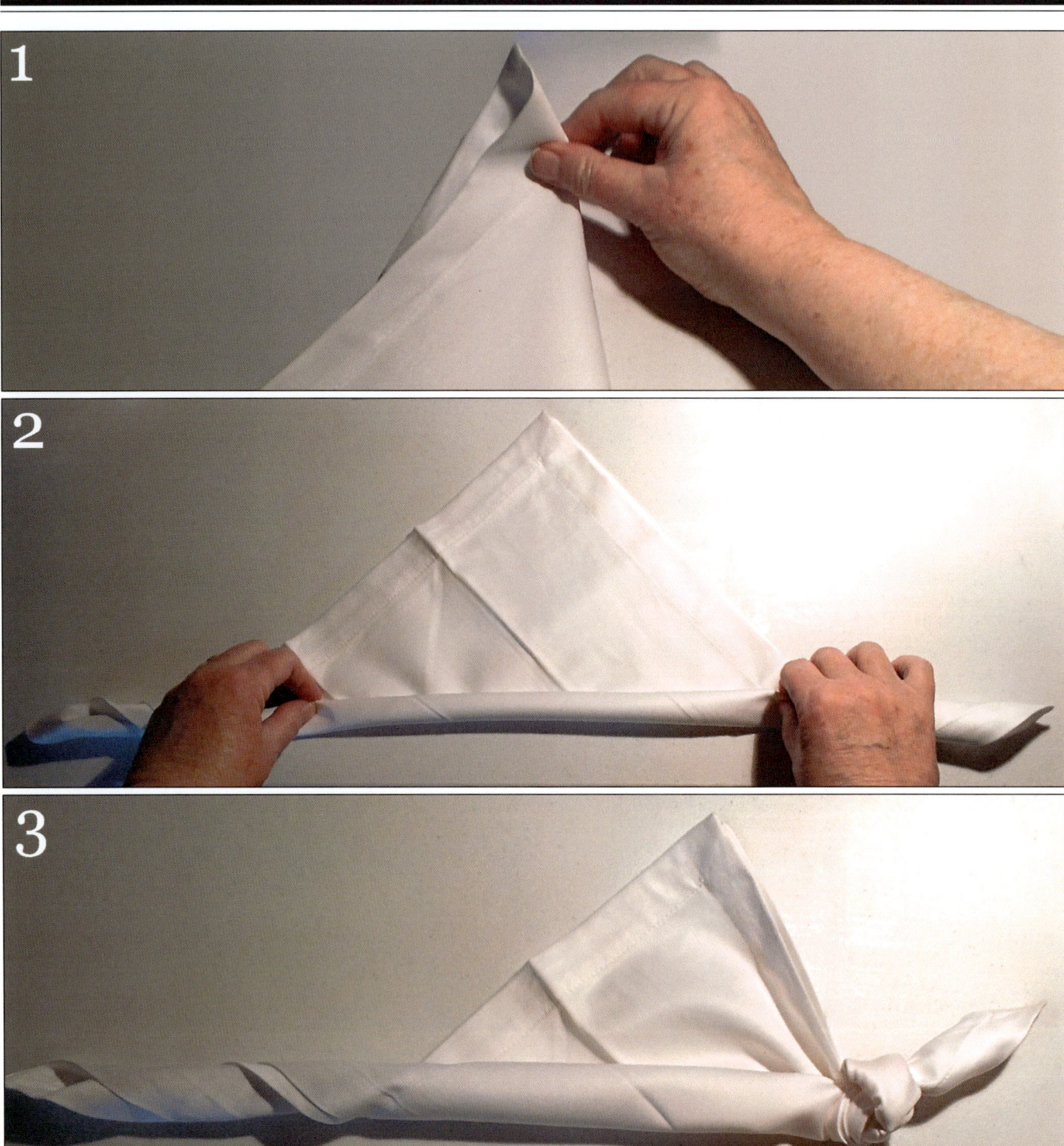

1. Fold the napkin in half, meeting opposite corners to form a triangle.

2. Roll the folded edge to a point about halfway between the folded side and the point of the triangle.

3. Tie the right edge of the rolled fabric into a loose slip knot to form a head and bunny ear.

4. Bring the left point of the rolled edge over and slip the point through the knot.

5. Bring the fabric pulled through the head knot around the front of the knot then pull it back through the knot again to form the second ear

6. Tuck the inner triangle into the body and tie the outer triangular piece into a small slipknot to form a tail.

The Squirrel

Napkin Tricks 13

1. Fold the napkin in half, meeting opposite corners to form a triangle.

2. Roll the folded edge to a point about halfway between the folded side and the point of the triangle.

3. Fold the roll in half.

4. Tie the two rolled ends into a slip knot that includes both rolls and some of the triangle.

5. Insert your index finger into the knot, inside the head. Unroll the roll to bring the squirrel's front arms up to his head. Put a little nut or candy in his arms to nibble on.

14 Napkin Tircks

The Snail

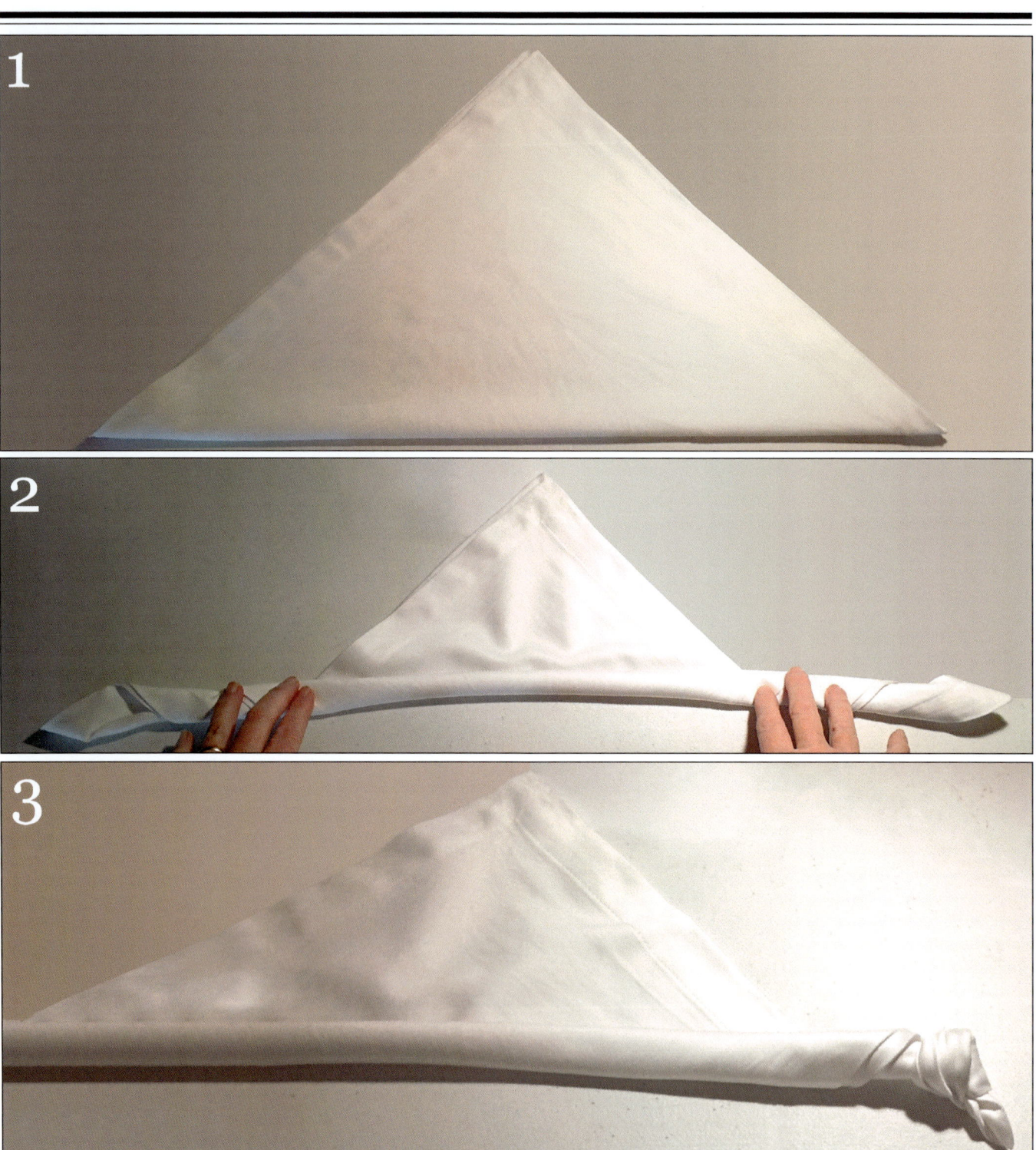

1. Fold the napkin in half, meeting opposite corners to form a triangle.
2. Roll the folded edge toward the point, leaving a small triangle of fabric.
3. Tie the top of the roll with a slipknot to form the head.

16 Napkin Tircks

4. Beginning at the end opposite the head, roll the napkin to form a flat circle with the triangle flaps sticking out.

5. Pull the top, outer triangle back over the roll and tuck into the coil between the last two layers of the roll.

6. Repeat step 5 with the inner triangle to finish

Napkin Tricks 17

The Rose

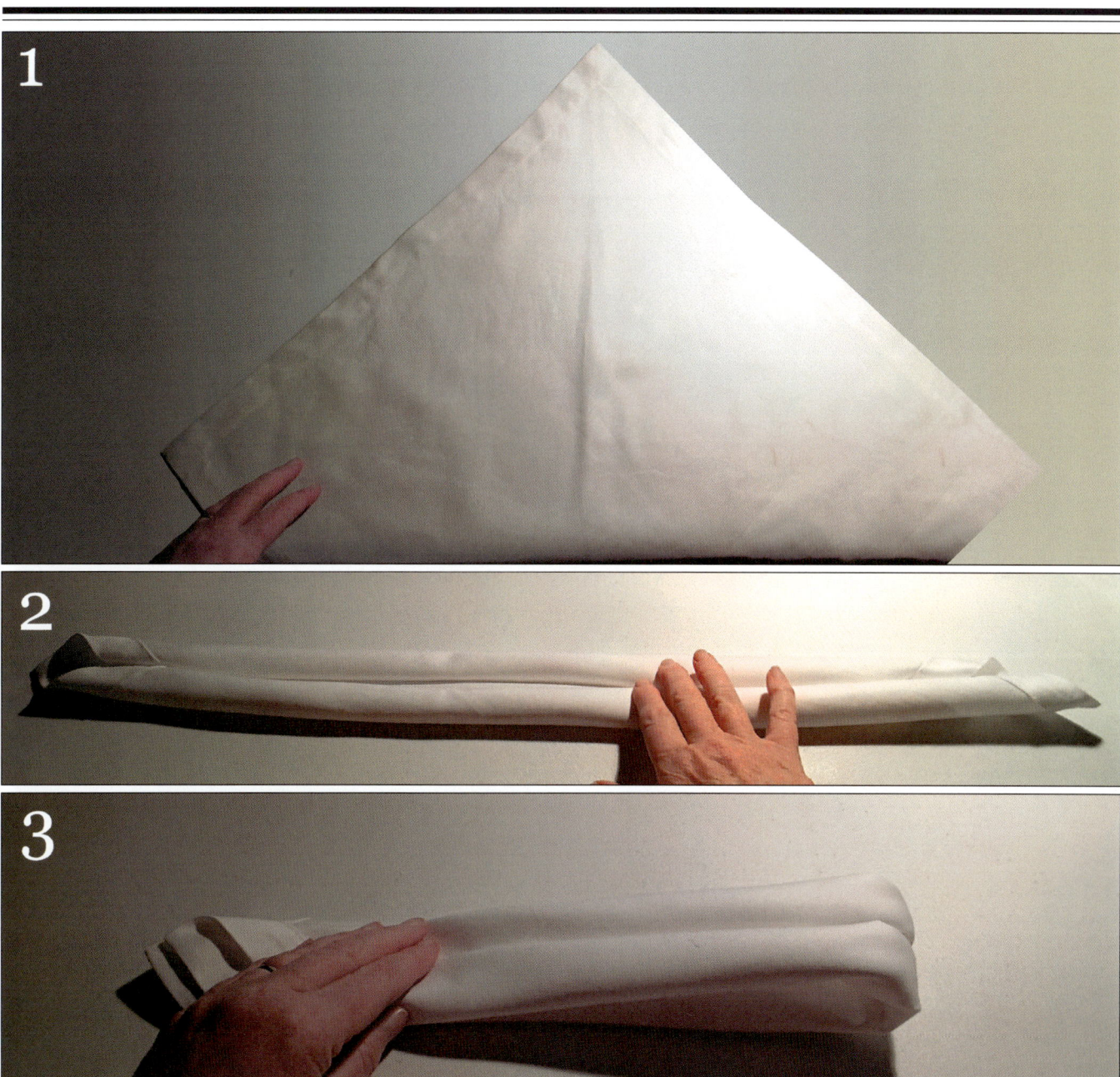

1. Lay the napkin out as a diamond.

2. Starting at the right corner, roll it to the center then roll the left side to the center.

3. Fold the napkin in half, matching top and bottom edges with the rolls facing to the outside.

4. Tie the top of the napkin rolls into a loose slip knot.

5. Unroll each of the two rolls below the knot to bring them up over the knot rosebud.

6. Tuck the front rolls into the back rolls where they meet at their ends.

7. To hold the rosebud, pinch the loose fabric at the bottom of the rosebud with your thumb and forefinger.

8. Hold the finished rose—or place it in a stemmed glass, on a plate or table.

The Dog*

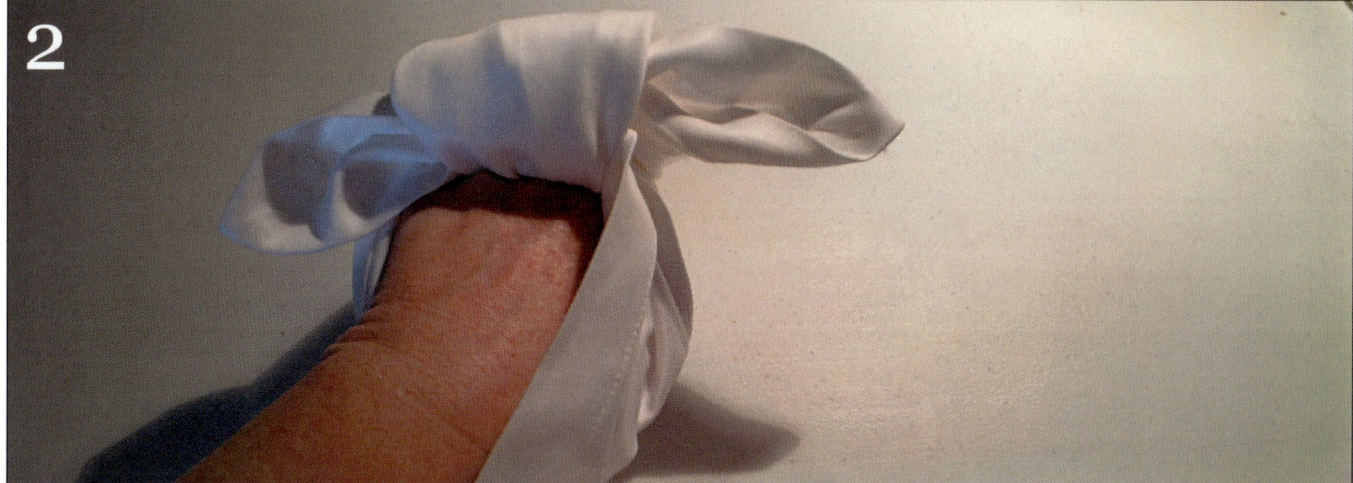

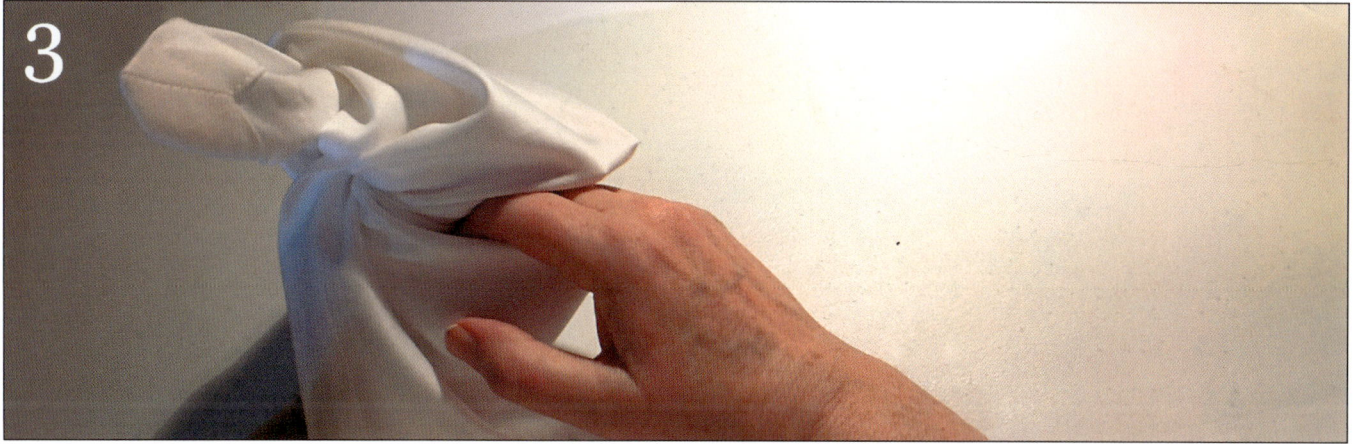

1. Lay the napkin out as a diamond. Grasp two opposite corners and tie them into a square knot.

2. Slip your hand into the napkin with the knot at the back of your hand. If the fabric is too loose, retie the knot. Grasp the top corner of the napkin, pull it straight back. Try to make the pulled top straight and neat by folding the edges under, then tuck the end under the knot between your fingers and the knot.

3. Tuck excess fabric into the opening created by your thumb and fingers to form a mouth. Shape the ears. Move the mouth to talk (bark) or eat.

Birdie in a Nest

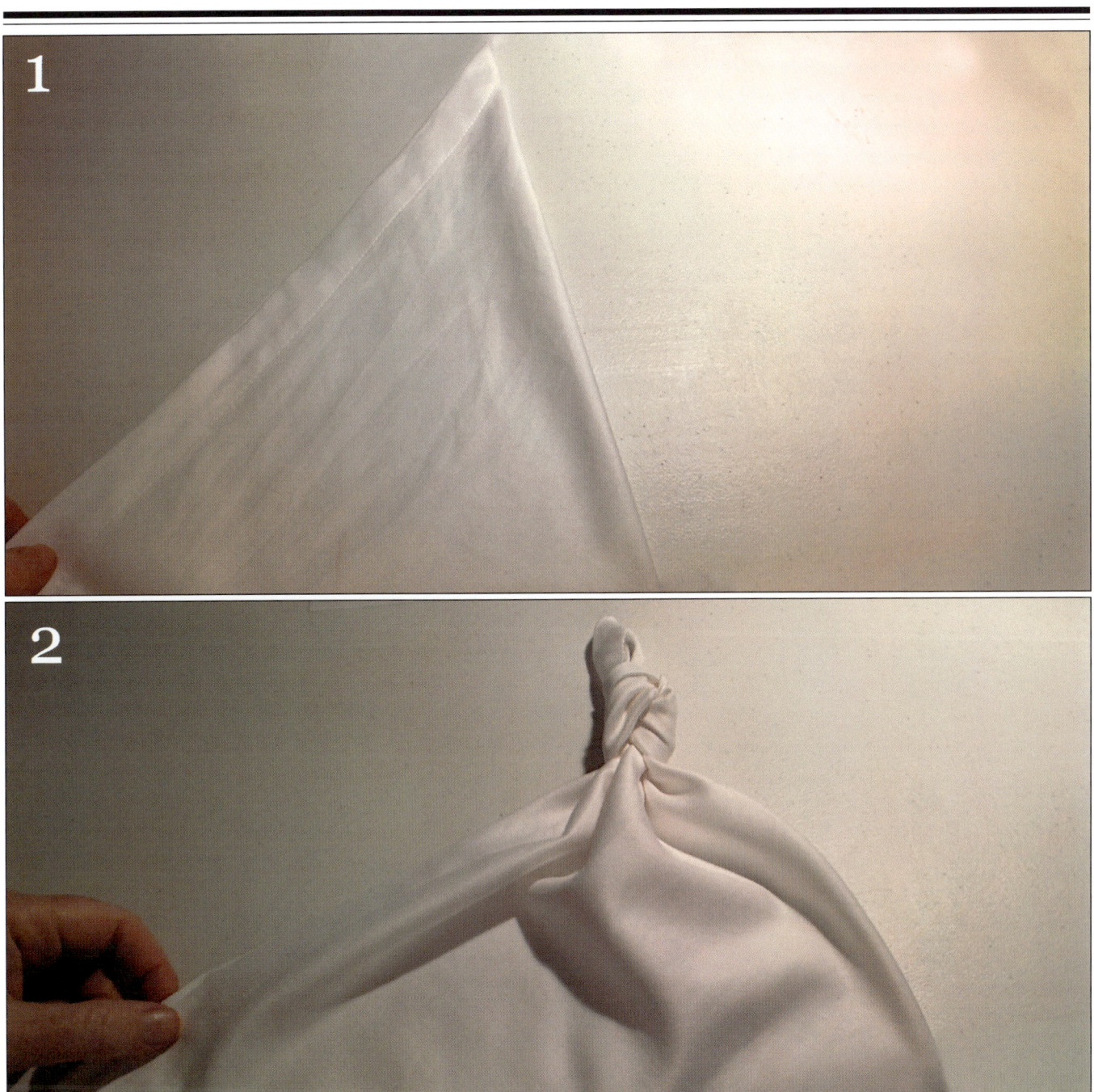

1. Lay the napkin out as a diamond. Fold the napkin in half.

2. Tie a loose slip knot in the top of the napkin, leaving a good piece of the napkin through the top of the knot. Later we will make the knot into the bird head and the piece into the beak.

Napkin Tricks 25

3. Open the napkin and roll in from the bottom toward the knot.

4. With the knot facing down, circle the roll with the roll facing outside. overlap the edges of the roll to create the nest.

26 Napkin Tircks

5. Continue to roll the overlapped rolled napkin toward the knot.

6. Tuck the top of the napkin back into the knot to create an open beak. Slip your index finger inside the knot through the bottom of the nest and wiggle to make the little bird head move.

The Fish

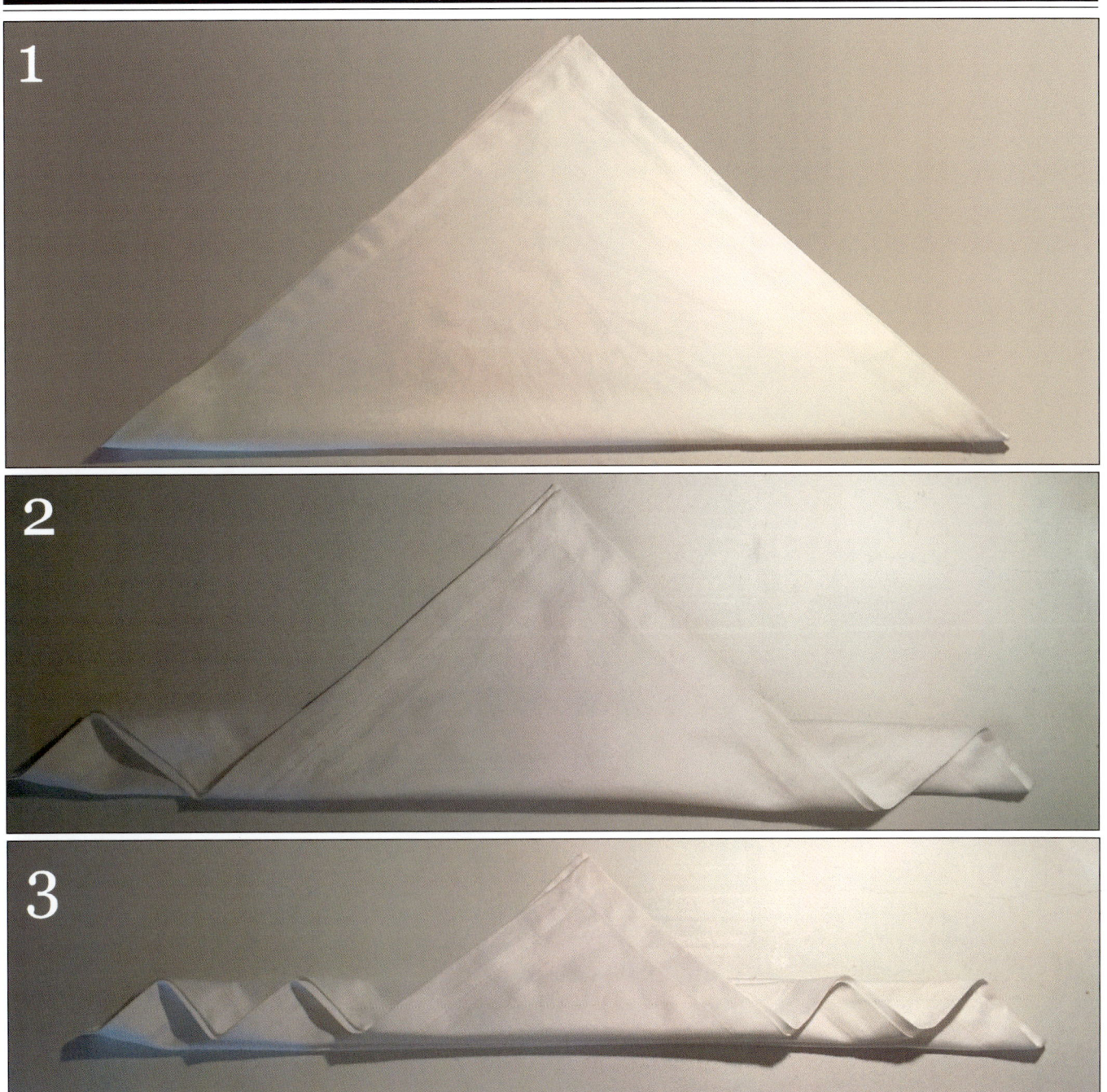

1. Lay the napkin out as a diamond. Fold in half to form a triangle.

2. Bring the point down to create a fold.

3. Continue moving that point up and down to create more folds.

Napkin Tricks 29

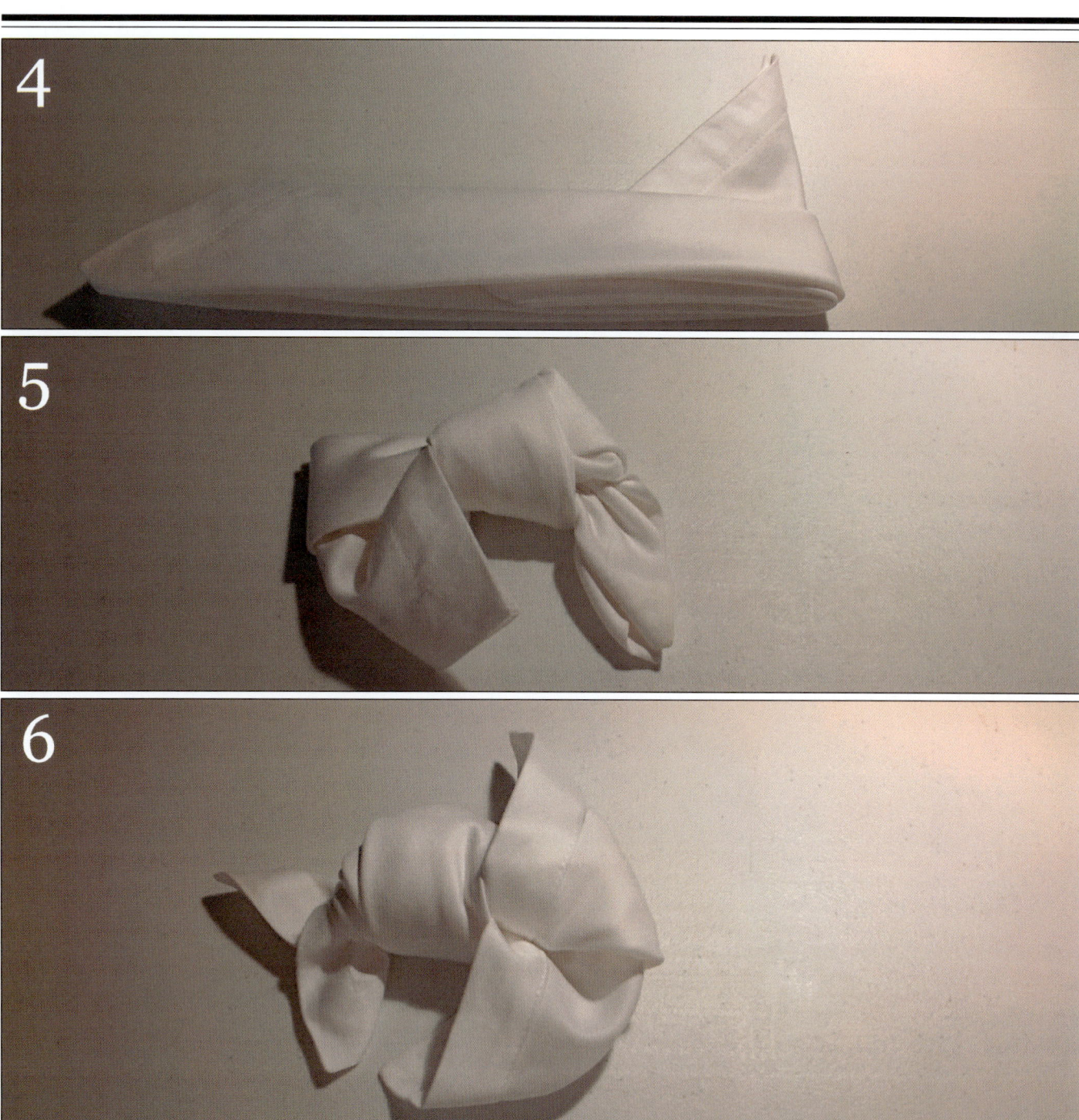

4. Fold the folded napkin in half.

5. Tie a slip knot, leaving the ends through the knot to become fins.

6. Pull the two triangles of fabric above and below the knot to become the head and mouth of the fish. Twist and position the tail fins.

30 Napkin Tircks

The Dancing Girl

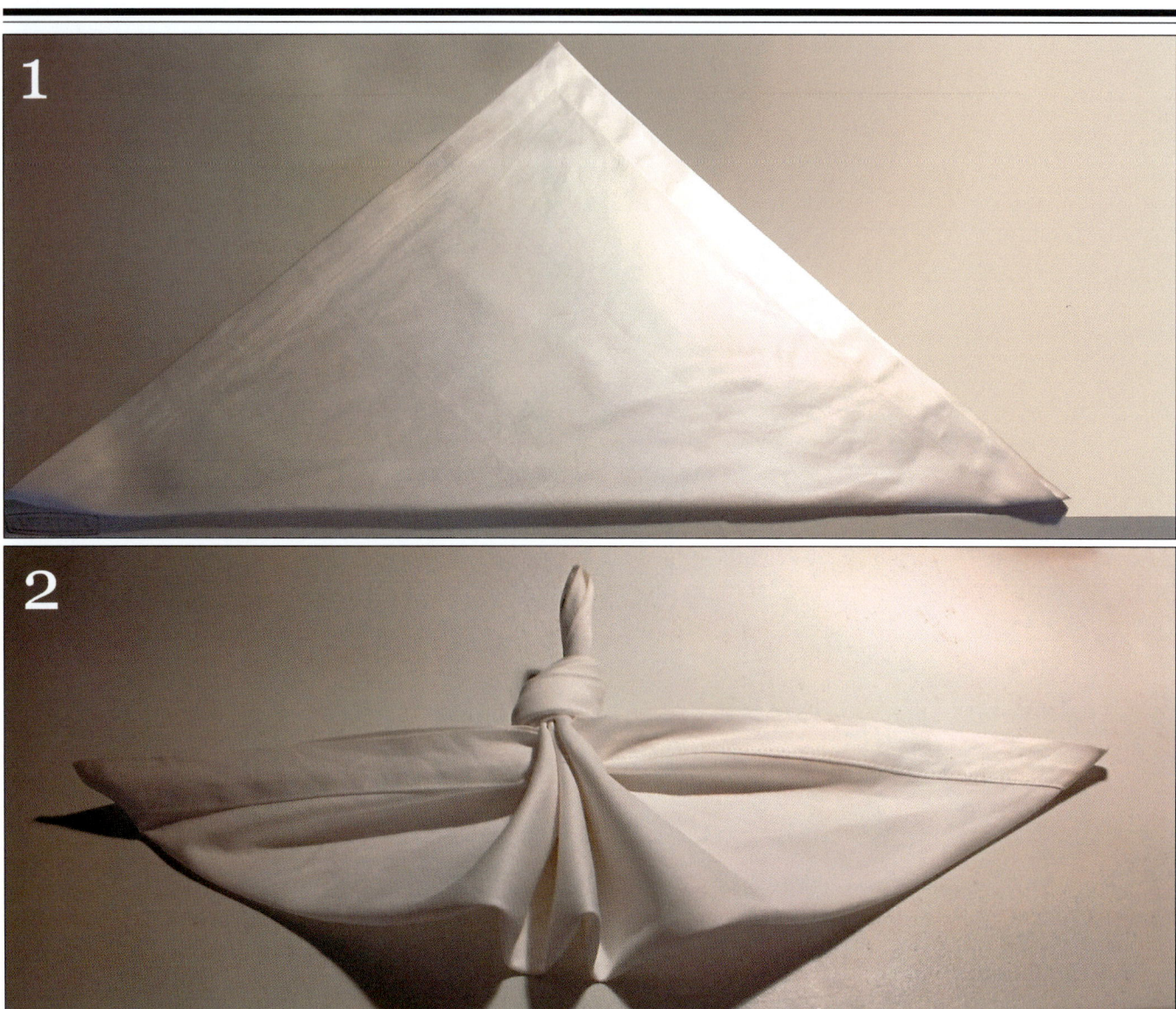

1. Lay the napkin out as a diamond. Fold in half to form a triangle with the apex pointing up.

2. Tie the top points into a slip knot, leaving enough ends to grasp when it's time to make her dance.

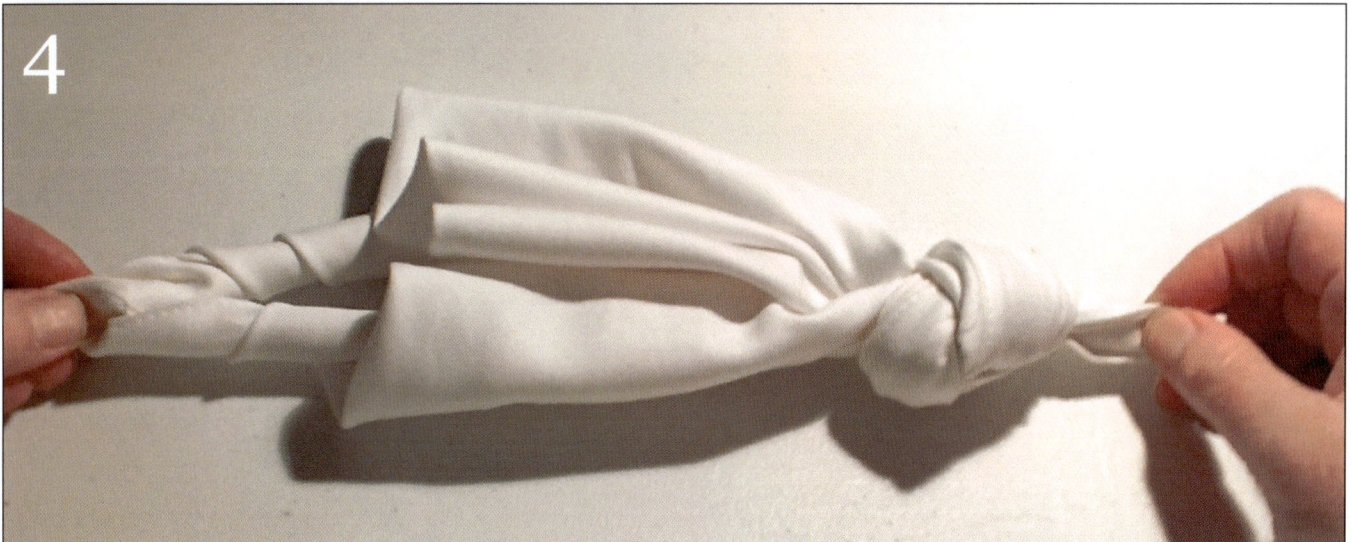

3. Grasp the opposite ends and spin the napkin to roll the napkin around itself to make her legs.

4. Bring those two ends together to hold between the thumb and forefinger of one hand. Arrange the loose fabric to form a body with the other hand. I rolled her skirt up in the main photo so you can see more of her legs.

5. Then grasp the end at the top of her head, hold her vertically and make her dance by moving your two hands slightly together and then away.

Dollie

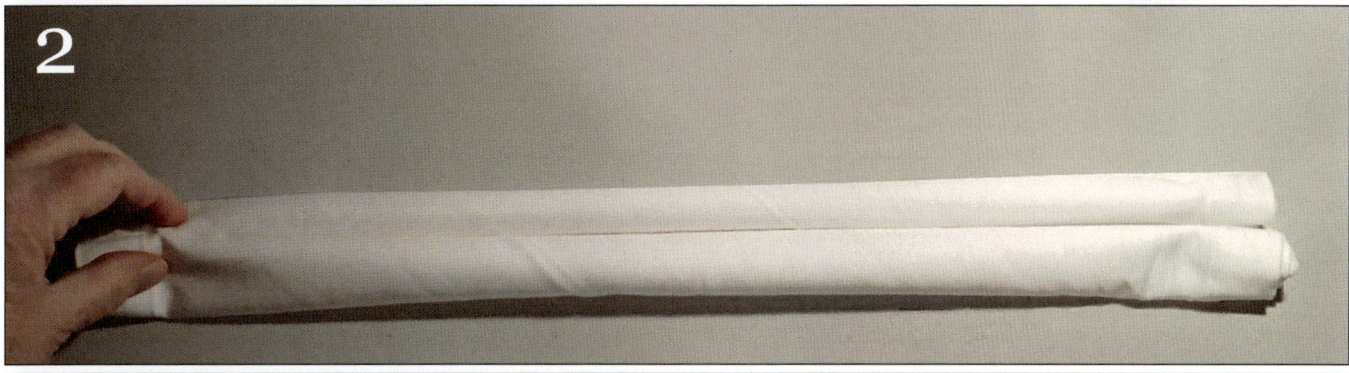
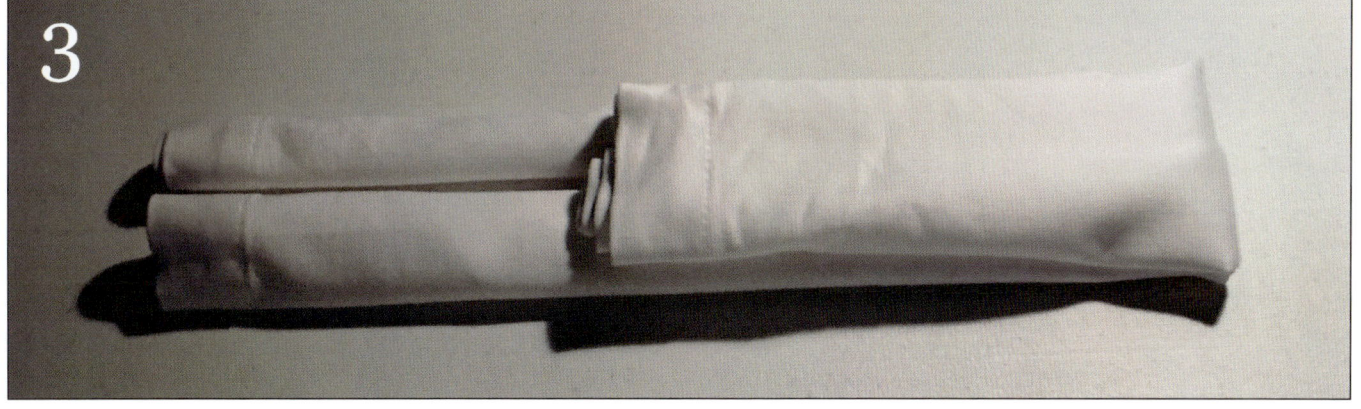

1. To begin, lay the napkin out as a square. Imagine a center line and roll one side to the middle.

2. Roll the other side to the middle.

3. Fold the rolled napkin toward you leaving about 1/3 of the rolled bottom showing

Napkin Tricks 35

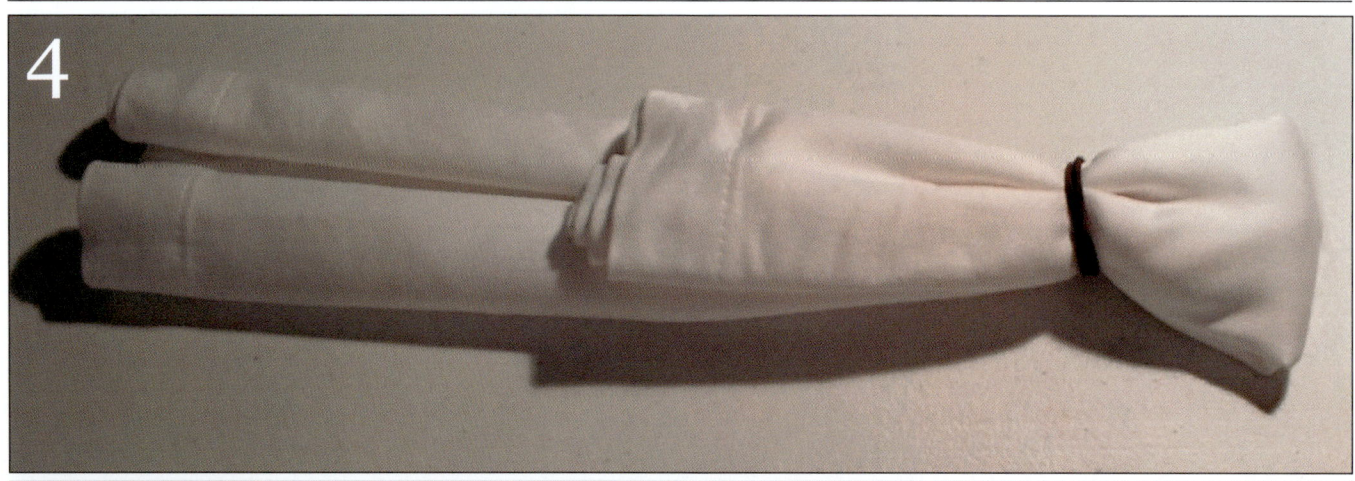

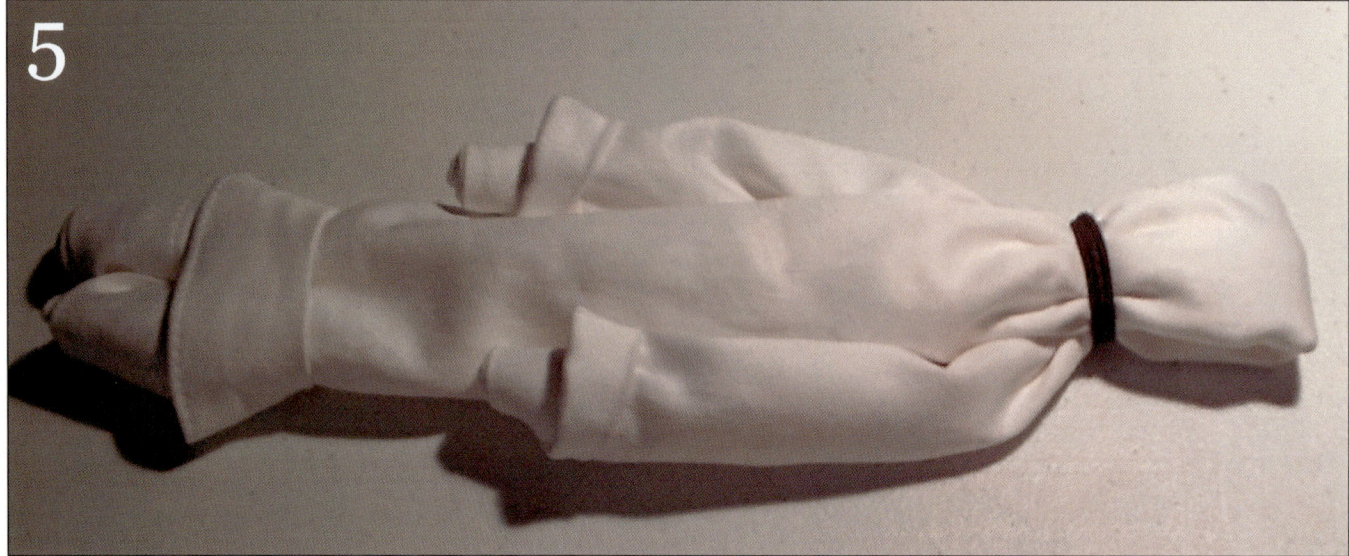

4. Wrap a rubber band (or a piece of straing, shoelace, or ribbon) around the top of the doll to create the head.

5. Flip the doll over. Unroll the arms to pull them out to the side. Turn up the hem of the dress and the sleeves if you want to see the hands and feet.

Twins in a Hammock*

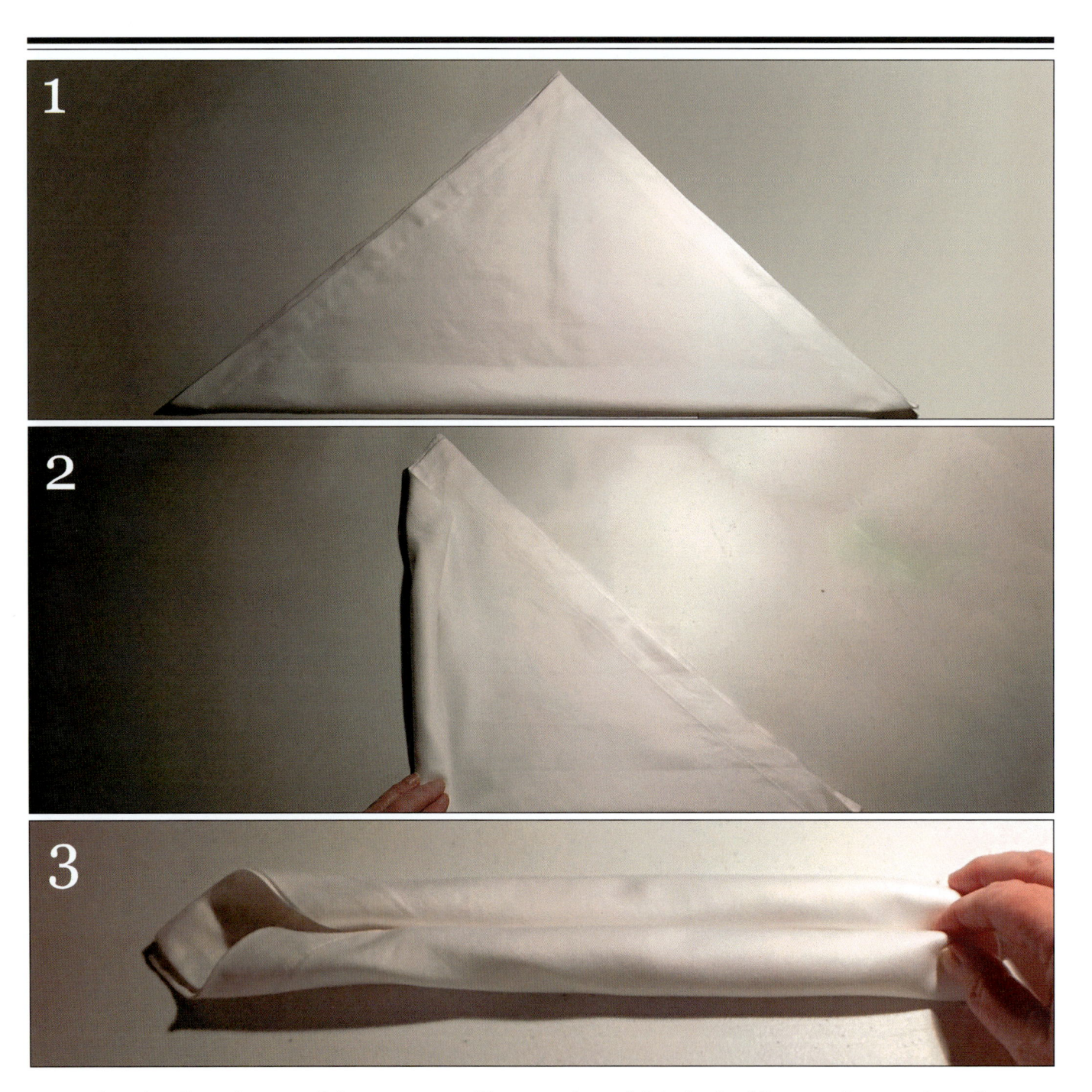

1. To begin, lay the napkin out as a diamond. Fold it in half to make a triangle.

2. Roll one side of the napkin to the middle. Turn the napkin so the points of fabric are to the left.

3. Roll the other side to the center, letting the two rolls meet. Now, holding the rolls so they don't unwind too much, grasp the bottom triangle of fabric and pull it under the "twins" and to the right to create a hammock.

The Butterfly

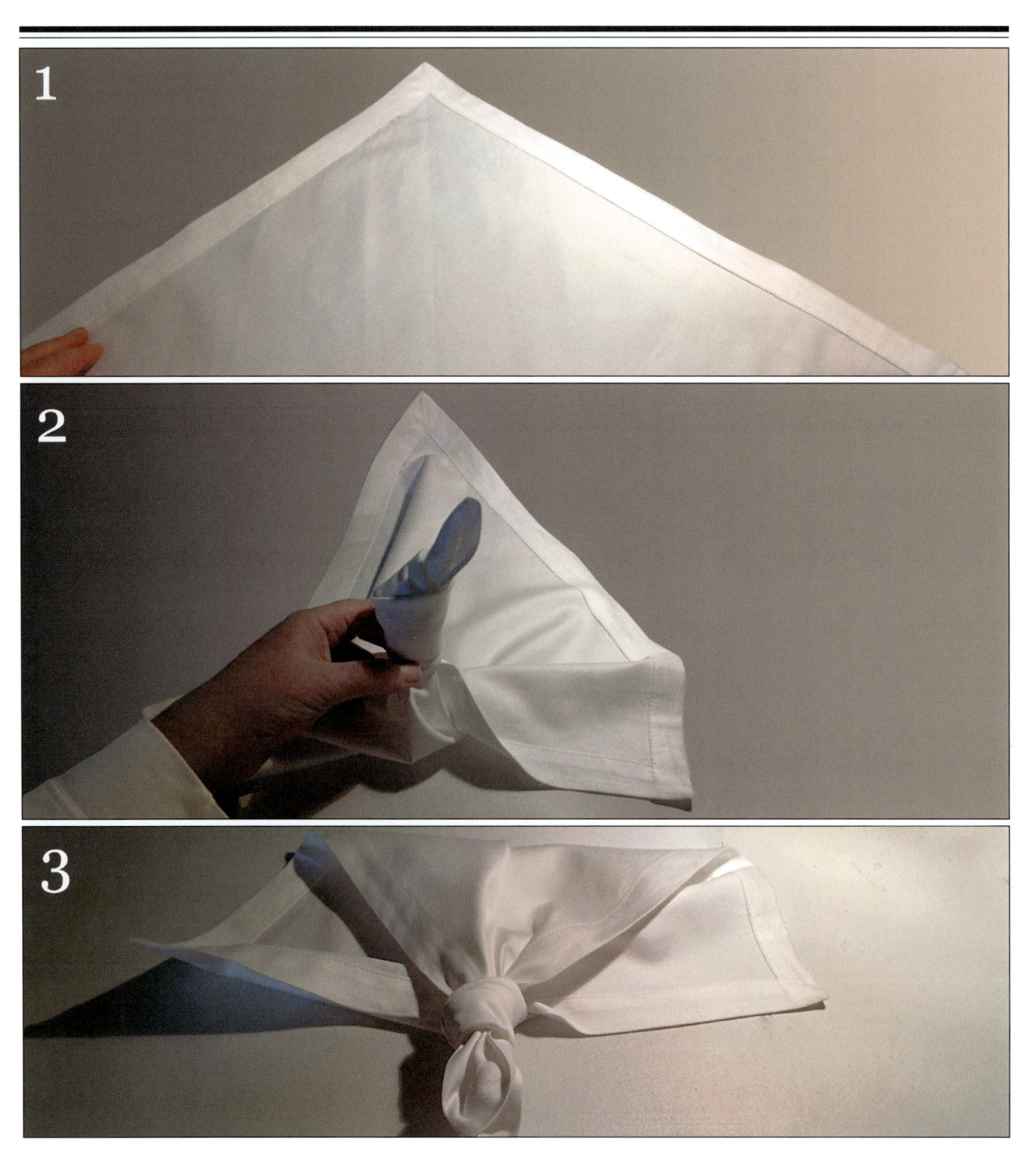

1. To begin, lay the napkin out as a diamond.

2. Grasp the bottom point and tie into a loose slip knot.

3. Take the top point and thread it through the knot. Pull the knot loop to tighten the knot, then adjust the length so that both flaps are even.

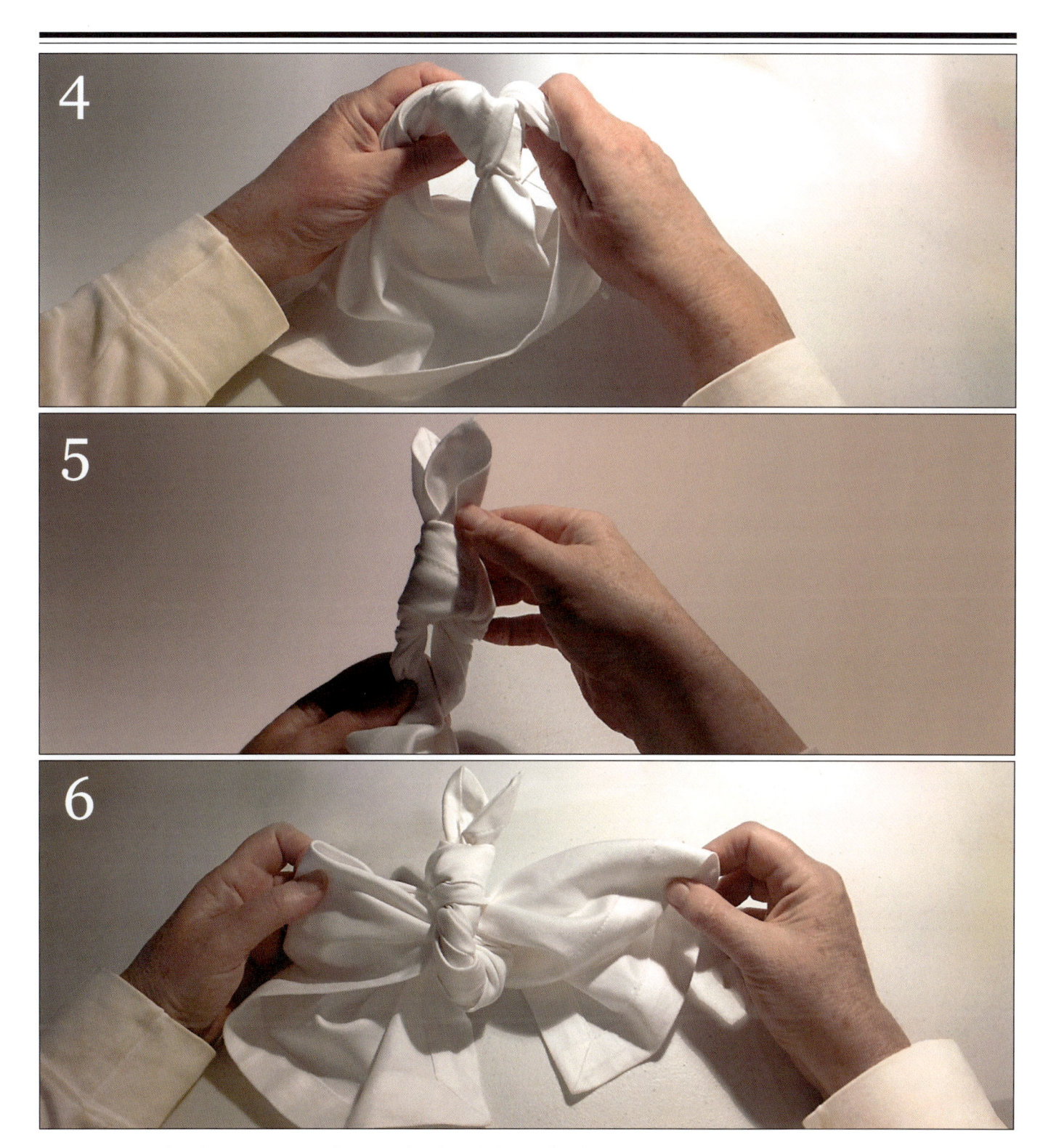

4. Rotate the knot once through the fabric hole created by the knot.

5. Grasp both ropelike sides and twist together once counterclockwise.

6. Take the left point and thread through the hole created by twisting the rope sides. Continue to pull the point through the hole until there is about equal amounts of fabric on each side, arrange to look like wings.

Napkin Tricks 41

Long-haired Girl

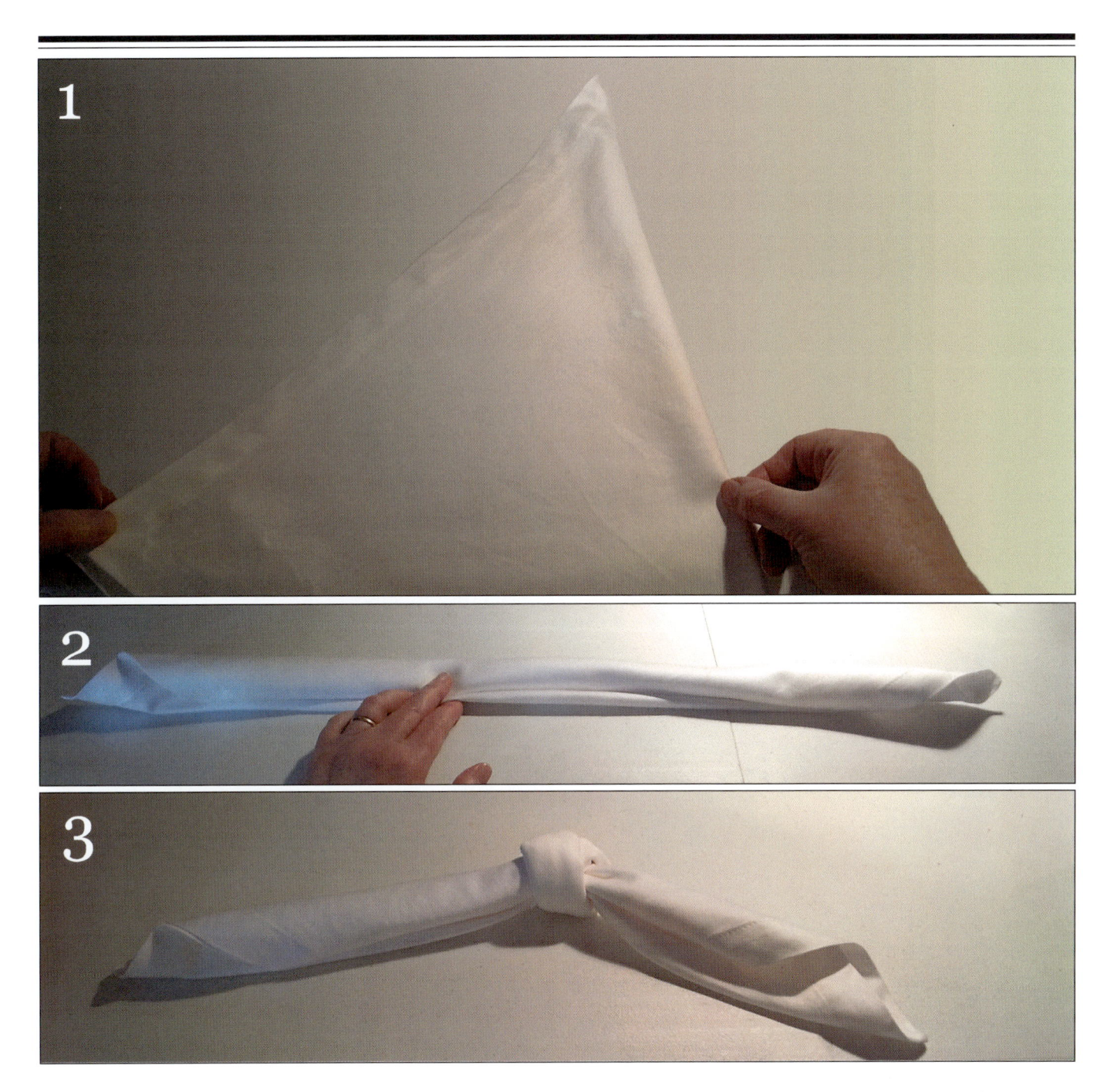

1. To begin, lay the napkin out as a diamond. Fold it in half with the triangle's apex pointing to the right.

2. Starting at the point, roll the fabric toward the folded side.

3. Tie a slip knot in the middle.

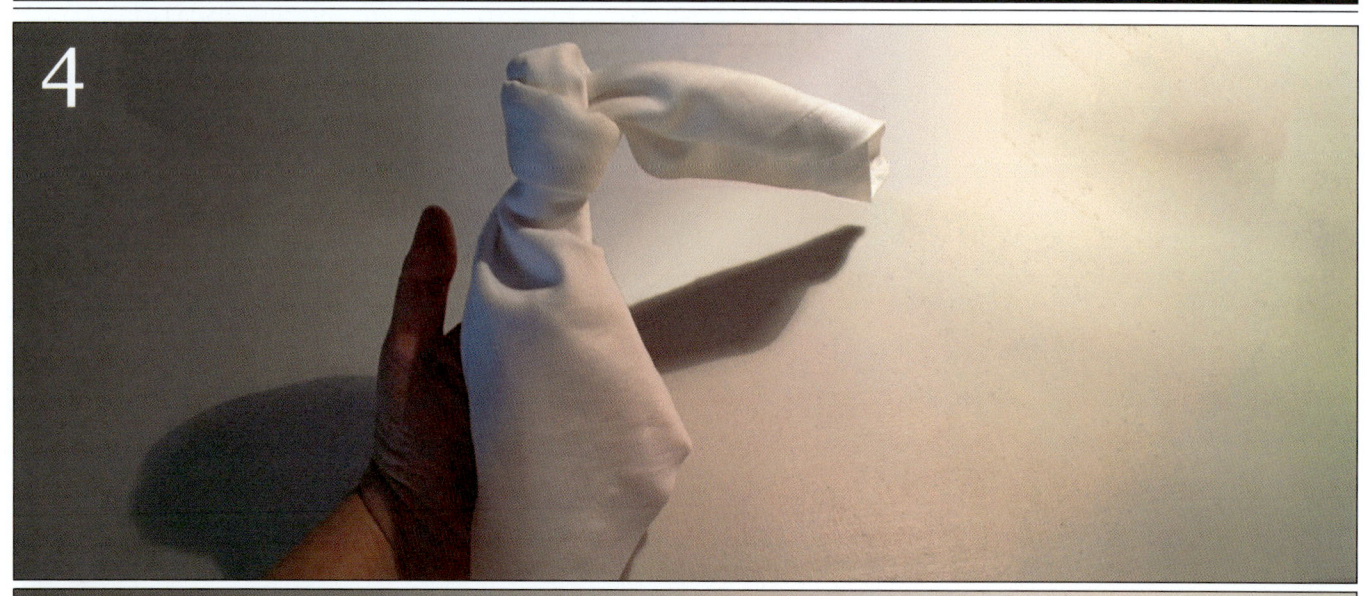

4. Insert your index finger into the knot.

5. Lift the top fabric, turn inside out and spread around the head to resemble hair. If you have a ribbon or band, tie it around the hair to finish.

44 Napkin Tircks

The Bunny Puppet*

1. To begin, lay the napkin out as a square. Grasp the top left and right corners and tie into a slip knot.

2. Adjest the ears to be an even length and to face forward. Insert your index finger into the knot.

3. Your puppet is ready! You can also slip a rubber band over your thumb and middle finger to create arms.

46 Napkin Tircks

Printed in Great Britain
by Amazon